THE BANTAM LIBRARY
of Culinary Arts™

Chocolate

JILL NORMAN

BANTAM BOOKS
TORONTO • NEW YORK • LONDON • SYDNEY • AUCKLAND

CHOCOLATE

A BANTAM BOOK/PUBLISHED BY ARRANGEMENT WITH
DORLING KINDERSLEY LIMITED

PRINTING HISTORY
DORLING KINDERSLEY EDITION
PUBLISHED IN GREAT BRITAIN IN 1989

BANTAM EDITION/MAY 1990

EDITOR GWEN EDMONDS
DESIGNER MATTHEWSON BULL
PHOTOGRAPHER DAVE KING

ART DIRECTOR STUART JACKMAN

LIBRARY OF CONGRESS CATALOGING-IN-PUBLICATION DATA
NORMAN, JILL.
CHOCOLATE:
THE CHOCOLATE LOVER'S GUIDE TO COMPLETE INDULGENCE /
JILL NORMAN. — BANTAM ED.
P. CM. — (THE BANTAM LIBRARY OF CULINARY ARTS)
"DORLING KINDERSLEY EDITION PUBLISHED IN GREAT BRITAIN 1989" — T.P. VERSO
INCLUDES INDEX.
ISBN 0-553-05740-5
1. CHOCOLATE. 2. COCOA. 3. CHOCOLATE PROCESSING. 4. COOKERY (CHOCOLATE)
I. TITLE. II. SERIES.
TX415.N66 1990
641.3'374—DC20
89—6839   CIP

BANTAM BOOKS ARE PUBLISHED BY BANTAM BOOKS, A DIVISION OF BANTAM
DOUBLEDAY DELL PUBLISHING GROUP, INC. ITS TRADEMARK, CONSISTING OF THE
WORDS "BANTAM BOOKS" AND THE PORTRAYAL OF A ROOSTER, IS REGISTERED IN
U.S. PATENT AND TRADEMARK OFFICE AND IN OTHER COUNTRIES. MARCA
REGISTRADA. BANTAM BOOKS, 666 FIFTH AVENUE, NEW YORK, NEW YORK 10103.

PRINTED AND BOUND IN HONG KONG
0 9 8 7 6 5 4 3 2 1

C O N T E N T S

THE DISCOVERY
OF CHOCOLATE

*I*N TRACING THE HISTORY of *chocolate we must bear in mind the fundamental difference between its various uses, as a drink, a flavoring, and a sweetmeat or candy. Each has a different story, and that of cocoa as a drink is by far the oldest. The story of drinking chocolate began in tropical South America, where the cocoa tree has grown wild for thousands of years and where successive Indian cultures were well aware of its properties. The Toltec and the Itzá knew and used cocoa, but the Maya were the first to cultivate it, very successfully: from the early seventh century they established a flourishing trade from plantations in the Yucatán peninsula and even introduced the cocoa bean as a unit of intertribal currency.*

European involvement in the story began in 1502, when Columbus brought the first cocoa beans to Spain – and nobody knew what to do with them. Twenty years later

16th century engraving of Aztec women preparing cocoa

A swizzle stick, used to froth the xocotlatl; it is carved from a single piece of wood

Montezuma, the last Aztec emperor, introduced Hernán Cortés to a sustaining drink he called *xocotlatl*. This is a contraction of two Nahuatl words meaning fruit and water. Montezuma's drink was a cold and rather bitter concoction made of roasted cocoa beans crushed to a paste and steeped in water, then thickened with cornflour. Spices, vanilla and sometimes honey were added to make the broth palatable. Bernal Díaz noted in his eye-witness account (*The Conquest of New Spain*) that "they brought him in cups of pure gold a drink made from the cocoa plant, which they said he took before visiting his wives." Cortés observed not so much the implied aphrodisiac properties but the drink's value in building up resistance and fighting fatigue. "A cup of this precious drink permits a man to walk for a whole day without food" he reported to his king. He learned about picking and processing the fruit and the preparation of the drink itself – and on his next voyage in 1528 he planted cocoa beans in Haiti, Trinidad and Fernando Po.

American Indian with chocolate pot and cup

THE CHOCOLATE
DRINK IN SPAIN

*Y*OUNG CHARLES V, *the new king of Spain and even newer Roman emperor, was greatly taken with the novel drink, and in the households of the Spanish nobles various refinements were invented to take away the bitterness of the cocoa with sugar, honey, spices and above all with vanilla, expensive concoctions made entirely from scarce imported ingredients. Whatever the recipe, the drink was originally served cold and rather thick, worked up to a froth with the Aztec swizzle stick (now called a molinet).*

Sometime during the 16th century chocolate became a hot and more liquid drink. It came to be poured from a pot resembling that used for the other exotic new drink of the period, coffee. The difference was the molinet which protruded through a hole in the lid of the chocolate pot. The cups in which chocolate was served also differed from coffee cups, in being appreciably taller.

16th century Peruvian silver chocolate cup and plate

The process of preparing the cocoa itself was being refined in the monasteries which established a monopoly in the retailing of the small dried tablets. Larger quantities of the raw beans were brought in, not only from Mexico but from the plantations established in the West Indies and on the African coast. Everywhere the Spanish empire spread, cocoa plantations were introduced – from Venezuela

The Chocolate Service,
Luis Melendez

to the Philippines – and for a full century cocoa remained a lucrative Spanish monopoly. Rumors of the new chocolate craze spread quickly to other parts of Europe but the article itself remained out of reach of most. Extravagant claims were made for it: Like many similar fads, the drinking of chocolate cured all ills and provided no end of stamina and prowess.

ITS SPREAD THROUGH EUROPE

*F*RANCE WAS THE FIRST COUNTRY *outside Spain to succumb to the chocolate craze. In 1615 the Spanish princess Anne of Austria married the king Louis XIII, and among the gifts she brought was a box of the fabled Spanish cocoa cakes.*

The court was a little slow in following her enthusiasm, but during Anne's regency, after the death of her husband in 1643, her invitations "to chocolate" were regarded as high social privilege. When in 1660 another Spanish princess, Maria Theresa, came to wed Anne's son Louis XIV she brought more cocoa, and to a much more appreciative audience.

In France as in Spain, chocolate remained a luxury, the domain of the court and the wealthy. In other European countries where wealth was associated more often with trade than with the aristocracy, the pattern was different. Holland had poached on the Spanish trading routes from the early years of the 17th century. At first its fleet had paid scant attention to cocoa, but before long the Dutch were alerted to its value and Amsterdam became the most important cocoa port outside Spain. It retains its hold even now: some 20 percent of the world's cocoa beans pass through Amsterdam, and Holland is the biggest exporter of cocoa powder, cocoa butter and chocolate in the world.

French chocolate advertisement, c. 1830

18th century Spanish tiles, showing a serving girl with chocolate

Dutch cocoa tin, 1940s

From Amsterdam cocoa went to Germany, Scandinavia, even on the long overland route to Italy. The Italians refined the drink still further, and their chocolate masters were much in vogue in the rest of Europe. Austria originally got its cocoa direct from Spain when the would-be king Charles of Spain returned to Vienna to become the emperor Charles VI, in 1711 – and only in Austria did chocolate become a truly national drink. The simple reason for this was that the Austrian government did not overtax the stuff. Everywhere else cocoa had become a substantial source of revenue.

CHOCOLATE IN ENGLAND

Fry's cocoa advertisement, c. 1920

*C*OCOA *did not really come to England until the 1650s. In 1648 Thomas Gage, a Dominican who traveled widely in the Americas, had reported its use in the West Indies where, he said, "all rich or poor, loved to drink plain chocolate without sugar or other ingredients," and in 1655 the capture of Jamaica brought some well-established cocoa plantations into English hands.*

Two years after that, a Parisian shopkeeper advertised "an excellent West Indian drink called chocolate to be sold in Bishopsgate Street, in Queen's Head Alley, at a Frenchman's house, where you may have it ready at any time, and also unmade at reasonable rates." Thus, five years after the establishment of the first London coffeehouse, a formidable rival movement began.

Neither coffee nor chocolate were court drinks in England: both were sold, from the very beginning, in specialty shops – to take away or consume on the premises. Samuel Pepys had his first chocolate in 1662, and soon made it his regular "morning draft." The most prestigious chocolate houses, White's and the Cocoa Tree, were established toward the end of the century. The main English innovations in the chocolate drink were the addition of claret and egg yolk, making a sort of wine caudle, and (after about 1730) of milk instead of or in addition to water. Still the drink was a thick one, with egg or some starch (usually arrowroot) added to combat the excessive fattiness of

the cocoa.
And still the
drink was frothed up with
the old swizzle stick, in late 17th-
century England called a mill.
The real revolution in chocolate
drinking and the beginning of
chocolate eating was caused by a
Dutch chemist, Coenraad Van
Houten, who invented a press that
took most of the fat out of the cocoa
beans, and who developed a method
of alkalization (still known as "dutching") that neutralized
the acids and made cocoa more easily soluble.

THE CHOCOLATE EATING HABIT

*V*AN HOUTEN'S PROCESS, *patented by his father, Caspar, in 1828, resulted in a mass of more or less pure cocoa butter and a very hard cocoa cake that could be milled to a powder. This soluble cocoa powder opened the way for much wider use as a flavoring. The early 18th century had already seen some attempts at chocolate-flavored biscuits, but the bitter taste and grainy consistency had always been a handicap, and truly satisfactory confections such as the famous Sacher Torte of 1832 would not have been possible any earlier.*

Rowntree chocolate box, c. 1925

French advertisement, c. 1910

Cocoa butter provided the foundation for a whole new industry, the manufacture of eating chocolate. The richness of the butter may have been objectionable in the drink, but its softness made it the ideal basis for a sweet nibble. The melting point of cocoa butter is only marginally lower than human body temperature – it literally melts in the mouth. It would be a while, though, before eating chocolate did the same. Among the earliest producers to launch eating chocolate was the Bristol firm of Fry, cocoa manufacturers since 1728; their first chocolate appeared in 1847.

The most significant improvements were made in Switzerland, a country that had come late to the use of cocoa.

The first Swiss factory was established in 1819, but here (as everywhere else) the great early names are still with us, for chocolate certainly has bestowed on firms the longevity it was often claimed to give to the individual.

Henri Nestlé invented baby food and the condensed milk that formed its base, and Daniel Peter had been experimenting with the addition of milk to chocolate. In 1875 the two combined forces and gave the world its

French "Cat's Tongues" box with chocolates

first milk chocolate. Around the same time Rodolphe Lindt invented another way of making chocolate smoother and more melt-in-the-mouth. His process, known as "conching," made the chocolate paste finer-grained and fully homogeneous by means of granite rollers in a shell-shaped pot (*concha* is Spanish for shell).

THE CHOCOLATE-LOVING COUNTRY

HE NORTH AMERICAN COLONIES took to cocoa relatively late. In 1712 a Boston apothecary offered some for sale, and for a long time the trade remained in the hands of the apothecaries: the various cocoa mixes were part of their "confections."

The drink was taken for its medicinal, health-preserving and health-restoring properties and did not become the social pastime it was in the mother country from which, originally, its ingredients were imported. In 1755 the Botany Bay fleet started trading directly with the West Indies, bypassing the double Atlantic crossing and therefore was easily competitive in price and delivery time. Ten years later one James Baker and a recently arrived Irishman, John Hannon, converted an old waterpowered grist mill into the first North American cocoa factory.

The United States must be the most chocolate-conscious

country on earth, and certainly the one in which chocolate as a flavoring outstrips all other tastes in popularity. Nobody did more to bring this about than Milton Hershey, a cocoa manufacturer who was so taken with the German chocolate manufacturing machinery he saw in the Chicago Exposition of 1893 that he bought the entire exhibit and started experimenting with its use. In 1903 he built his first chocolate factory. Now, the Hershey bar is to "candy" what the Coca Cola bottle is to soft drinks. Hershey launched his first chocolate bar in 1894 and lived to see a version of it adopted as emergency rations for the American forces in World War II. Today the town of Hershey, Pennsylvania, has become a sort of chocolate theme park of Disneyland proportions.

Advertisement for Hershey's Kisses

25 million Hershey Kisses are wrapped every day

THE COCOA TREE

*F*ROM ITS ORIGINAL HOME *in tropical South America the cocoa tree has spread to the whole region between the 20th parallels, with the notable exception of central and eastern Africa, where the soil is too poor and the climate too dry for it.*

West Africa has the ideal conditions, around the Gulf of Guinea. The Ivory Coast, Ghana, Nigeria and Cameroon are the largest exporters now, followed by Brazil and Ecuador. The trees start bearing fruit after four years and their active lifespan easily reaches sixty. The dark-green leaves are quite large, often up to a foot (25–30 cm) long. Thousands of small

Cocoa plantation, 1933

Cocoa pod

pink flowers on short stalks grow directly out of the older wood of the trunk and the main branches all year long—but not more than twenty or thirty at a time will produce mature fruit (there are two crops a year). That fruit, the pod, is six inches by four inches. Ripening, it changes from green to a variety of colors—yellow, orange, red and purple. Inside the pod are the purplish cocoa beans, some thirty or forty of them, surrounded by a pale pink pulp.

Beans and pulp are fermented together, which turns the beans

Cocoa pod and section of tree

a dull red and develops their characteristic flavor. After fermentation the beans are dried in the sun and acquire their final "chocolate" color. In this form they are shipped to the manufacturing countries.

PROCESSING COCOA BEANS

*T*HESE DAYS, COCOA MANUFACTURING *is no longer carried out in its entirety by a single producer: Parts of the process have become a specialized business. Primary processors make what the trade calls "intermediate," the stages between the raw bean and the end product. Basically, these intermediates are cocoa mass (in earlier days called cocoa liquor), cocoa butter and cocoa powder.*

Nibs

Dried beans

When the dried beans reach the processing plant they are mixed into different blends according to their ultimate use. Then they are cleaned and cracked into a mixture of broken shells and hard kernels (called nibs) by centrifugal force. Shells and nibs are separated, and the nibs are now ready for roasting in huge rotating drums. Their color darkens and the flavor develops more fully. During roasting or immediately after it "dutching" is applied, if necessary (this depends on the intended use of the end product). Van Houten's original process used potash, but later manufacturers have developed their own methods. Finally, the roasted nibs are ground into a viscous substance called cocoa mass – the base product for all further stages of manufacture. If the cocoa mass is subjected to

Cocoa butter

Cocoa mass

very high pressure, cocoa butter (which accounts for more than half) is forced out, leaving a hard cocoa cake. The liquid cocoa butter is then purified and stored either as a

Cocoa crumb

liquid in temperature-controlled tanks, or as solid blocks. Both liquid and blocks can be shipped. The cocoa cake that forms the residue is crushed into rough pieces. These are stored until needed, when after further blending they will be pulverized in a grinding mill to any specific size grain. The finer the cocoa powder, the hotter it gets in this process. It is passed through cooling coils before being packed.

PROCESSING CHOCOLATE

*C*OCOA MASS IS THE BASIC INGREDIENT *for all forms of chocolate, but it needs a lot of manipulation and additions before it reaches the consumer. First of all it is mixed with a large quantity of sugar – as much as 40 to 60 percent, depending on the desired end product – and with flavorings such as vanilla or powdered milk to make milk chocolate. This mixture then goes through a rolling mill, which reduces the lumpy stuff to a fine-grained thin sheet of raw material.*

A selection of fine handmade chocolates

Suchard box, c. 1910

The next step is conching, originally also done with rollers but these days with rotating paddles in large vats. Conching usually takes two days or more, and during this time more cocoa butter is added to the mix until the right consistency is reached. The resulting hot liquid is stabilized in a tempering machine, which cools it to the right temperature for molding.

After the addition of ingredients like fruit and nuts, the paste is poured into molds that travel over a vibrating conveyer belt to force out air bubbles. When the chocolate is cool and solid the molds are inverted and the bars or other shapes travel down another conveyer to be packaged.

Small chocolates are made either by shaping a hard center and then coating it with chocolate, or by putting chocolate into hollow molds which are immediately inverted so that only a thin mantle adheres to the sides, then putting a filling in the hollow and closing the mold with another layer of chocolate.

21

CHOCOLATE CONFECTIONS

*F*RY'S CHOCOLATE CREAM *was the first filled bar on the market in the 1870s.* "Bonbons" *or chocolate-coated candies appeared a little earlier than that, but the most enduring ones were Hershey's Kisses of 1907 and Cadbury's Milk Tray selection launched in 1914. Candy bars consisting of layered centers with a chocolate coating were pioneered*

by Frank Mars in the 1920s.

The chocolate manufacturing industry goes on devising new and more marketable forms of its product – bars plain or filled, coated fruits and nuts, truffles, bonbons and the like.

All these attractive forms, and others made at home, go back to blocks of the basic ingredient: bitter, milk and white, or even orange-flavored confectioners' chocolate, available only from specialty shops.

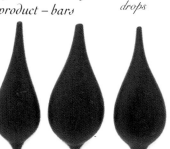

Chocolate drops

Confectioners' chocolate

Unsweetened baking chocolate

For flavoring desserts, cakes and other dishes requiring only small amounts, a convenient form is the chocolate morsel sold in supermarkets or the small bar of dark "baking chocolate" (still usually imported from France).

Small chocolate drops, plain and milk

Recipes

*All recipes serve 4, but some
(such as cakes and tarts)
will serve more.*

VANILLA SUGAR

Vanilla sugar is useful for many desserts and cakes. Simply put a *vanilla bean* in a jar of *superfine sugar* and add more sugar as you use it. Vanilla beans retain their flavor for a long time and give foods a much better taste than artificial vanilla extract.

TO MELT CHOCOLATE

Cut the chocolate in slivers with a sharp, heavy knife and put them in a bowl. Bring a pan of water to boil, remove it from the heat and set the bowl of chocolate on top. Make sure the bottom of the bowl is not touching the water. Cover with a lid to keep in the heat. Stir the chocolate occasionally as it melts and after 10 minutes or so, when it is no longer lumpy, stir continuously until very smooth and fluid.

For dipping, leave the chocolate to cool a little so that it begins to thicken, but keep the bowl over the pan of water while using it. If the chocolate hardens while dipping, melt again over hot water.

CHOCOLATE CHARLOTTE

5 oz/150 g butter
2/3 cup/125 g sugar
6 oz/175 g unsweetened chocolate
1 egg yolk
1/2 cup/125 ml milk
1/2 cup/125 ml rum or brandy
1/2 cup/125 ml water
3/4 lb/375 g lady fingers.

Beat 4 oz/125 g butter and the sugar together until pale and light. Melt 4 oz/125 g chocolate as described opposite. Beat the egg yolk and milk together. Stir the egg and milk mixture into the chocolate and then add the butter and sugar mixture. Beat for several minutes until light and fluffy.

Dilute the rum with the water and soak the lady fingers. Oil a charlotte mold thoroughly and line the bottom and sides with lady fingers. Cover the bottom with a layer of chocolate cream, then add a layer of fingers. Continue to fill the mold, finishing with a layer of lady fingers. Put a weighted plate on top and refrigerate for 12 hours.

Turn out onto a plate. Melt the remaining chocolate, stir in the last piece of butter until it is smooth and pour the chocolate over the charlotte.

CHOCOLATE SOUFFLE

5 oz/150 g unsweetened chocolate
4 oz/125 g butter, softened
2/3 cup/125 g superfine sugar
6 eggs
3 tablespoons bread crumbs
2 tablespoons flour, sifted

Melt the chocolate with 2 tablespoons of water. Beat the sugar into the butter until pale and creamy, then add the egg yolks, one at a time, beating to a frothy cream. Stir in the bread crumbs and flour and then the chocolate. Whisk the egg whites until stiff and fold them in.

Pour into a buttered soufflé dish and stand the dish in a pan of hot water. Bake in a preheated oven, 375°F, 190°C, for 50 minutes to 1 hour.

SIMPLE CHOCOLATE MOUSSE

4 oz/125 g unsweetened chocolate
4 eggs

Melt the chocolate over hot water. Stir until smooth. Separate the eggs and when the chocolate has cooled a little, beat in the yolks. Whisk the whites until stiff and fold in. Pour into small pots or a glass serving dish and chill in the refrigerator for at least 12 hours.

Variations

Melt the chocolate with 2 tablespoons of strong coffee.

Add 2 tablespoons of brandy, whisky or Grand Marnier before adding the egg whites.

Add 1/3 cup/60 g ground almonds and 4 tablespoons heavy cream before adding the egg whites.

RASPBERRY AND CHOCOLATE DESSERT

1/2 lb/250 g raspberries
1 1/4 cups/300 ml heavy cream
2 tablespoons sugar
2 tablespoons kirsch
6 oz/175 g unsweetened chocolate, grated

Whip the cream, sugar and kirsch until the mixture holds soft peaks. Stir in three quarters of the grated chocolate. Put the raspberries in a glass serving bowl, spoon over the cream and sprinkle the remaining chocolate on top. Chill before serving.

CHOCOLATE MARQUISE

4 oz/125 g unsweetened chocolate
½ cup/50 g confectioners' sugar
3 oz/75 g butter, softened
3 eggs

Melt the chocolate and stir well until smooth. Beat in the sugar and then the butter cut into small pieces. Remove from the heat and stir in the egg yolks, one at a time. Beat the egg whites until stiff and fold into the chocolate mixture.
Rinse a loaf tin with cold water and fill with the marquise. Chill for at least 12 hours.
To turn out, dip the tin briefly in hot water. Serve with whipped cream.

CINNAMON CHOCOLATE CREAMS

2 oz/50 g unsweetened chocolate
1¼ cups/300 ml light cream
2 eggs
1 egg yolk
½ teaspoon ground cinnamon
2 tablespoons sugar

Melt the chocolate. Bring the cream to the boil and pour into the chocolate, stirring well. Beat the eggs, yolk, cinnamon and sugar together and slowly pour in the chocolate and cream.
Pour the cream through a cheesecloth-lined sieve into small ramekins and put them in a pan of hot water. Cover the whole with a sheet of foil and bake in a preheated oven, 325°F, 160°C, for 20–30 minutes. Test with a skewer to see that the creams are set. Set aside to cool then refrigerate.

CHOCOLATE ICE CREAM

2½ cups/600 ml milk or light cream
¼ cup/50 g cocoa
½ cup/100 g superfine sugar
3 egg yolks

Stir the cocoa into the milk and bring gently to the boil. Beat the sugar and egg yolks together until pale, then gradually beat in the boiling milk. Pour the mixture back into the pan or into the top of a double boiler and stir for 10 minutes over very low heat until the custard is thick enough to coat the back of the spoon.

Pour into a bowl to cool, stirring occasionally to prevent a skin forming, then turn into an ice cream machine and freeze.

Variations

Before freezing add
2–3 oz/50–75 g finely
chopped crystallized ginger.

3 tablespoons whisky or brandy.

3 tablespoons Grand Marnier or Cointreau and a tablespoon of grated orange peel.

2 oz/50 g chocolate chips.

CHOCOLATE LIEGEOIS

1 recipe chocolate ice cream (above)
½ cup/150 ml whipping cream
1 tablespoon confectioners' sugar
cocoa

Chill 4 tall glasses. Take the ice cream out of the freezer 20 minutes before making the

chocolate liegeois. Whip the cream until doubled in volume, gradually adding the sugar. Fill each glass almost to the top with ice cream, then top with a large swirl of cream. Sprinkle with cocoa and serve.

CHOCOLATE AND CHESTNUT PARFAIT

1/2 cup/150 ml water
2/3 cup/125 g sugar
4 egg yolks
4 oz/125 g unsweetened chocolate
3 tablespoons milk
1 1/4 cups/300 ml whipping cream
4 oz/125 g chestnut purée

Bring the water and sugar to the boil, boil for 3 minutes, then remove from the heat. Beat the egg yolks well and pour the syrup onto them, stirring briskly until the mixture cools. Melt the chocolate in the milk, stir until smooth, then beat into the egg mixture, a little at a time. Whip the cream until it holds light peaks. Fold the cream and chestnut purée into the chocolate cream.
Pour into a soufflé dish and freeze for 6 hours. To turn out, plunge the dish briefly into a bowl of hot water.

CHOCOLATE TORTE WITH WHITE CHOCOLATE TOPPING

¾ cup/175 g ground walnuts or pecans
5 tablespoons bread crumbs
6 oz/175 g unsweetened chocolate, grated
¾ cup/175 g superfine sugar
⅓ cup/50 g flour
1 tablespoon baking powder
pinch of salt
4 oz/125 g butter, softened
2 tablespoons brandy
6 large eggs, separated
¼ pint/125 ml double cream
3 oz/75 g white chocolate

Butter a 9-in springform pan, line the bottom with waxed paper or baking parchment and butter the paper.

Mix together the first seven ingredients and work in the softened butter. A mixer or food processor will do the job quickly. Add the brandy and egg yolks and mix until thoroughly blended.

Whisk the egg whites until stiff and fold them into the batter. Pour the mixture into the pan and bake in a preheated oven, 350°F, 180°C, for 1 hour or until a tester inserted in the middle comes out clean. Let the torte cool in the pan on a wire rack. Turn it out and store in the refrigerator.

To serve, decorate the torte with ½ cup/125 ml whipping cream beaten with 3 oz/75 g melted and cooled white chocolate.

ᴀNNA SACHER'S SACHER TORTE (1883)

"*5 oz/140 g dark, unsweetened chocolate*
3½ oz/100 g butter
⅔ cup/140 g superfine sugar
4 egg yolks
4 egg whites
⅔ cup/70 g flour
325°F, 170°C/60 minutes

Set the chocolate in the oven on a plate to warm and melt gently. Cool slightly. Beat the butter and the sugar in a bowl until pale and fluffy, then beat in the chocolate. Beat in the egg yolks one at a time and combine well. Whip up the egg whites to a stiff snow and mix lightly into the chocolate mixture with a metal spoon. Fold in the sifted flour carefully, taking care not to loose any air. Have ready an 8½-inch springform pan, greased and floured; pour in the mixture, rap the pan on the counter to dispel any air pockets, and bake in the preheated oven. Cool on a wire rack and then cover with a plain chocolate icing; you may like to coat the cake first with apricot jam to insulate it against the chocolate."

Barbara Maher, *Cakes*, 1982

CHOCOLATE CAKE WITH AMARETTI

2 oz/50 g butter
3 eggs, separated
6 amaretti, crushed
2 oz/50 g cocoa
1/3 cup/75 g sugar
1 1/4 cups/300 ml light cream

Cream the butter and egg yolks until pale, then stir in the amaretti, cocoa, sugar and cream. Whisk the egg whites until stiff and fold them in. Butter a small loaf pan, pour in the mixture and stand the pan in a baking pan filled with hot water. Bake in a preheated oven, 425°F, 220°C, for 40 minutes. Leave to cool in the pan on a wire rack. The cake becomes firm as it cools.

CHOCOLATE TART

1/2 lb/250 g shortcrust pastry
4 oz/125 g unsweetened chocolate
1/3 cup/75 g superfine sugar
4 eggs
1 1/4 cups/300 ml whipping cream

Line a 9-in or 10-in flan pan with a loose base with the pastry. Prick the bottom with a fork. Melt the chocolate and stir until smooth. Remove from the heat and mix with the sugar, eggs and cream. Pour the mixture into the pastry case and bake in a preheated oven, 400°F, 200°C, for 25–30 minutes. Serve cold.

GÂTEAU AU CHOCOLAT

"The ingredients required for
this simple sweet are:
*a quarter of
a pound of grated unsweetened
chocolate, a quarter of a pound of
superfine sugar, two ounces of
ground almonds, two ounces of
butter, one ounce of flour and
three eggs.*

The mold should
be of the crown kind. Put the
butter in a basin and stir it till it
becomes frothy, then add, in
turn, first the yolks of the eggs,
then the other ingredients,
finishing by the whites whipped
to a stiff froth. Butter some
waxed paper, put it in the mold,
pour in the mixture and cook in
a slow oven for about three-
quarters of an hour."

Marcel Boulestin,
A Second Helping, 1925

CHOCOLATE CAKE

6 oz/175 g unsweetened chocolate
6 oz/175 g butter
²/₃ cup/125 g superfine sugar
1 cup/125 g potato flour
4 eggs, separated

Melt the chocolate. Cream the
butter and sugar until pale, then
stir in the chocolate. Add the
potato flour and egg yolks,
alternating them and beating
well. Whisk the egg whites until
stiff and fold in.
Pour into a buttered 8-in
cake pan and bake in a
preheated oven, 375°F, 190°C,
for 30–35 minutes. Cool on a
wire rack.

BROWNIES

4 oz/125 g butter
4 oz/125 g unsweetened chocolate
2 cups/250 g vanilla sugar (see p. 24)
4 eggs
1 cup/125 g self-rising flour
1 cup/125 g walnuts, chopped

Melt the butter and chocolate together. Beat the eggs and sugar until light and pale, then stir in the chocolate mixture. Sift the flour over the bowl and fold in. Stir in the nuts. Grease and flour a shallow square baking pan, pour in the batter and bake in a preheated oven, 350°F, 180°C, for 25–30 minutes.

Leave to cool in the pan, then cut into squares.

CHOCOLATE MACAROONS

3 oz/75 g unsweetened chocolate
4 oz/125 g vanilla sugar (see p. 24)
5 oz/175 g hazelnuts, skinned and
ground (p. 39)
1/2 teaspoon ground cinnamon
(optional)
2 egg whites

Melt the chocolate, then remove from the heat and stir in the other ingredients to make a soft paste. Line a baking sheet with edible rice paper or baking parchment, roll the mixture into small balls with your hands and put them on the paper. Flatten the tops with a knife and bake in a preheated oven, 350°F, for 12–15 minutes. Break off excess rice paper or peel off the baking parchment (if the macaroons stick, wipe the underside with a wet cloth) and cool on a wire rack.

CHOCOLATE CHIP COOKIES

4 oz/125 g butter
2 oz/50 g vanilla sugar (p. 24)
2 oz/50 g soft brown sugar
1 egg
1 cup/125 g flour
1/2 teaspoon baking soda
pinch of salt
4 oz/125 g chocolate chips

Beat together the butter, sugars and egg until fluffy. Sift in the flour, baking soda and salt and mix well. Stir in the chocolate chips. Grease a cookie sheet and drop teaspoonfuls of the mixture onto it, leaving plenty of room for the cookies to spread. Bake in a preheated oven, 375°F, 190°C, for 8–10 minutes. Remove from the oven while the centers are still slightly soft and leave on the cookie sheet for 5 minutes before cooling on a wire rack.

Variation

Use 4 oz/125 g white chocolate, cut into small pieces, to replace the chocolate chips, and add 2 tablespoons cocoa to the flour.

Nut and Raisin Balls

1/4 cup/50 g blanched almonds
1/4 cup/50 g skinned hazelnuts (p. 39)
1/3 cup/75 g raisins
1/4 cup/50 g dried apricots
4 tablespoons rum or brandy
5 oz/150 g milk chocolate

Chop the nuts, raisins and dried apricots together quite finely—a food processor does the job well. Stir in the rum. Melt the chocolate, stir until smooth, then mix with the nuts and fruit. Let it cool slightly, then drop teaspoonfuls onto a sheet of waxed paper or foil. Leave for 2 hours to harden.

Hazelnut Balls

3/4 cup/175 g hazelnuts, skinned and ground (p. 39)
1 3/4 cups/175 g confectioners' sugar
4 oz/125 g chocolate, grated
3 tablespoons rum
2 egg yolks
1/3 cup/175 g cocoa

Mix the nuts, sugar and chocolate in a bowl and stir in the rum and egg yolks. Blend thoroughly. Put the cocoa in a shallow tray. Take teaspoonfuls of the mixture and roll into balls with your hands, then roll the balls in the cocoa and store in the refrigerator. They will keep for 2 to 3 days.

Variation
Use milk chocolate and omit the rum.

Chocolate-Coated Peel

Dip long pieces of candied orange peel for their whole or half their length into the chocolate.

CHOCOLATE-COATED MARZIPAN

Make the marzipan sweets the day before coating with chocolate to make sure they are quite dry, otherwise the chocolate will not stick.

3¾ cups/375 g ground almonds
3¾ cups/375 g confectioners' sugar, sifted
2–3 tablespoons rose water
1 egg white, lightly beaten
a few drops almond extract (optional)
½ lb/250 g dark dipping chocolate

Mix the almonds and sugar thoroughly in a bowl. Stir in the rose water, egg white and almond extract and knead by hand until the mixture coheres and forms a smooth paste. Shape into a ball and wrap in plastic wrap. Stored in the refrigerator, the marzipan will keep for up to 2 months. Either shape the marzipan into small balls by hand or roll out like pastry and cut into shapes. Melt the chocolate. Line a cookie sheet with waxed paper or foil. Spear the pieces of marzipan on a fork or skewer and drop one at a time into the chocolate. When coated all over, lift out, shaking off excess chocolate, and let them set on the tray, then serve on a dish.

CHOCOLATE-COATED GINGER

Good quality crystallized ginger can be coated in the same way, but cut the ginger first if the pieces are large.

Truffles

8 oz/250 g unsweetened chocolate
¼ cup/50 ml whipping cream
3 oz/75 g butter, softened
2 tablespoons superfine sugar
2 egg yolks
2 tablespoons kirsch
¼ cup/50 g cocoa

Melt the chocolate with 1 tablespoon of water. Stir until smooth, then add the cream, butter and sugar, a little at a time. Remove the bowl from the pan of hot water, and when it has cooled a little, stir in the egg yolks and kirsch. Beat well until the mixture is smooth and shiny. Let cool for several hours. Put the cocoa in a small bowl. Form the mixture into small balls and dip them in the cocoa powder.

Store the truffles in the refrigerator, but take out 15 minutes before serving. They will keep for 2 to 3 days.

Variations

Use whisky, rum, brandy or another liqueur instead of kirsch.

Add 1–2 teaspoons grated orange rind with whisky or an orange-flavored liqueur.

Add 2 teaspoons ground coffee beans with brandy.

Coat the truffles in icing sugar or a mixture of cocoa and cinnamon, in grated chocolate or chocolate vermicelli.

CHOCOLATE-COATED NUTS

Walnuts, pecans, blanched almonds and hazelnuts are all good coated in chocolate. Hazelnuts should be roasted first in a low oven for about 10 minutes, then rubbed in a dish towel to remove the skins. Make sure the nuts are very dry before putting them into the chocolate.

SPANISH CHOCOLATE

4 oz/125 g unsweetened chocolate
1³/4 cups/450 ml milk
1/2 teaspoon ground cinnamon
2 eggs

Grate the chocolate into the milk, add the cinnamon and heat gently, stirring frequently, until the chocolate dissolves. Whisk the eggs lightly and add them. Beat until the chocolate thickens, but do not let it boil.

VIENNESE CHOCOLATE

1/2 cup/125 ml whipping cream
1 tablespoon confectioners' sugar
4 oz/125 g unsweetened chocolate
1³/4 cups/450 ml milk

Whip the cream until doubled in volume, adding the sugar gradually. Chill while making the chocolate. Grate the chocolate into the milk and heat gently, stirring, until the chocolate dissolves. Pour into cups and top with a swirl of chilled cream.

INDEX

ACKNOWLEDGMENTS

The publishers would like to thank the following people:

JACKET
· PHOTOGRAPHY ·
DAVE KING

· TYPESETTING ·
WYVERN
TYPESETTING LTD

· ILLUSTRATOR ·
JANE THOMSON

DESIGN
· ASSISTANCE ·
SUE CORNER

· REPRODUCTION ·
COLOURSCAN
SINGAPORE

*The publishers would like to thank the following
for permission to use photographs and objects:*

4 LH. PHOTO: JEAN-LOUP CHARMET, PARIS   **5** PHOTO: JEAN-LOUP CHARMET, PARIS

6 MRS MABEL MARAÑON BURNS   **7** PRADO, MADRID, PHOTO: ARXIU MAS

8 PHOTO: JEAN-LOUP CHARMET, PARIS

9 MUSEO DE ARTES DECORATIVAS, MADRID, PHOTO: ARXIU MAS

10 MARY EVANS PICTURE LIBRARY   **11** GERALD SATTIN LTD, LONDON.

12 LH PHOTO: JEAN-LOUP CHARMET, PARIS

12, 13 RETROGRAPH ARCHIVE COLLECTION, LONDON.

15 HERSHEY FOODS CORPORATION, PENNSYLVANIA, USA

16 RETROGRAPH ARCHIVE COLLECTION, LONDON   **17** CADBURY-SCHWEPPES RESEARCH CENTRE

18, 19 CADBURY-SCHWEPPES RESEARCH CENTRE   **18** BODLEIAN LIBRARY, OXFORD

21 PHOTO: JEAN LOUP CHARMET, PARIS

20 BOTTOM: RETROGRAPH ARCHIVE COLLECTION, LONDON

22 LH. BODLEIAN LIBRARY, OXFORD

ELINOR BREMAN AND LAURA CLIPSHAW FOR PREPARING FOOD.

CYNTHIA HOLE FOR PICTURE RESEARCH.